THE IMITATION OF CHRIST

THE IMITATION OF CHRIST

Thomas à Kempis

RELEVANT BOOKS

Published by RELEVANT Books
A division of RELEVANT Media Group, Inc.

www.relevantbooks.com
www.relevantmediagroup.com

Design by RELEVANT Solutions
Cover design by Anna Melcon
Interior design by Ben Pieratt, Jeremy Kennedy, Anna Melcon, Aaron Maurer

For information or bulk orders:
RELEVANT MEDIA GROUP, INC.
100 SOUTH LAKE DESTINY DR., STE 200
ORLANDO, FL 32810
407-660-1411

Library of Congress Control Number: 2005911200
International Standard Book Number: 0-9776167-1-1

08 09 10 8 7 6 5 4 3 2

Printed in the United States of America

CONTENTS

INTRODUCTION

Something deep is born in solitude. You sense it when you talk to someone who has hiked the Appalachian Trail or run a marathon or practiced the cello for the last sixteen years. Or someone who has spent time at a monastery.

My friend Jim was a monk for twenty-five years before leaving that life to pursue a career as a storyteller. During all those years of prayers and chants and midnight vigils, Jim learned a quiet calmness, a sense that this moment is enough and that worry and regret are thieves of peace.

I've been to monasteries several times on four-day silent retreats. After about twenty minutes I've had all the deep spiritual insights I can take. I start frantically looking around for a computer to check my email. I wouldn't make a very good monk.

___

When Thomas Hemerken was twenty-one, he was accepted into the Augustinian Monastery at Saint Agnes in the Netherlands. He spent the next seventy-one years as a monk, copying the Bible, reading, praying, and writing about Jesus. He led a pretty simple life, but his insights have inspired millions. We know him today as Thomas à Kempis, or "from Kempen," since he took on the name of his hometown. And my guess is when you read this guy's words, you'll see for yourself what choice fruits silence and contemplation can produce.

Even with my less-than-restful pace, I've learned incredible lessons from this quiet man who died in 1471. And I'm not the only one. *The Imitation of Christ* has been translated into more than fifty languages and reprinted more than two thousand times since it was first published in 1418. Some people say it's the second-most-read book of all time, trailing only the Bible. Who knows? Any way you cut it, though, Thomas has helped a lot of frenzied people like me unpeel some of the busyness in our lives and learn simple truths about imitating Jesus.

What strikes me most about Thomas is his honesty. He pulls out a scalpel and performs surgery on his own soul, laying bare his fears, envies, desires, and convictions. His time alone with God taught him both courage and humility—a rare combination. And his writing bears this out. Somehow he's able to say all the things most of us dread to admit but know are true as soon as we read them.

For example, he wrote, "He who seeks anything but God alone and the salvation of his soul will find only trouble and grief, and he who does not try to become the least, the servant of all, cannot remain at peace for long." Most of us know that clawing our way toward wealth and influence won't bring peace, only more heartache—yet we do it anyway. And most of us know that seeking God halfway or living just to please ourselves inevitably leads to trouble and grief. We know this, but until we're reminded of it, it doesn't always hit home. We need someone like this medieval monk to remind us of these things we already know.

I first read this book early in my Christian walk fifteen years ago, and even now, whenever I reread it, I'm struck by its simple yet profound truths: the life of faith is one of simplicity, obedience, and humility. As straightforward as all that sounds, I'm still just beginning to understand it.

Thomas sees the road to an authentic spiritual life as one paved with cobblestones of confession. This isn't a safe little book. You'll be challenged to be courageous and honest. As you read, you'll see that Thomas believes the true imitator of Jesus isn't the one who has accomplished the most, but rather the one who has surrendered the most. After all, the greatest saints aren't those who've learned the most, prayed the most, served the most, built the biggest churches, or handled the most snakes—rather, the greatest saints are the ones who are the least self-absorbed. And by the time you're done, I think you'll agree that Thomas from Kempen is one of God's spiritual first-stringers.

Sometimes people refer to Thomas as one of the Christian mystics; that sounds very cool to some and a little freaky to others. What's a mystic, anyway? Does it mean you sell all you own, shave your head, and spend the rest of your life on a mountaintop in Tibet doing Tai Chi? Well, maybe. But not always. From my experience, I'd say that mystics tend to emphasize encountering God rather than just studying Him. They would say that the road to God isn't theology but love, that the most remarkable believers aren't the best-informed but the least proud, and that mystery is just as important as truth when it comes to relating to God. And if that stuff makes someone a mystic, Thomas à Kempis would be one. And I'd be one too, or at least I'd want to be.

God wants us to live the most risk-enlivened, love-enriched life possible. And for most of us, the only way to leave our self-enclosed lives is to be loved out by Jesus, as awkward and disturbing as that can be. This book will lead you toward that kind of mystical life.

So here's my advice as you explore this book: Nibble at it. Take time to reflect on it. This isn't like a novel you devour in one sitting. Savor Thomas' words. As you do, you'll sense the depth of his spiritual understanding. The simple truths expressed here are powerful enough to transform you in real and lasting ways. So give them some time and space to do their work in your soul. And as you read, let God's Spirit touch your spirit— sometimes with a lover's caress, and sometimes with a father's disciplining hand. Be ready for both.

To Thomas, the "Jesus life" is one of faith rather than sight, simplicity rather than extravagance, moderation rather than indulgence, sacrifice rather than acquisition, and risking the ways of God rather than settling into the soul-numbing security of the ways of the world.

If it's true that the depth of our prayers isn't measured by the number of our words but by the humility of our hearts, then Thomas' prayers must have been as deep as the night and as rich as the dawn. Let the lessons he learned in solitude speak to you and create the space in your soul for some healthy Spirit-fruit to grow in your own life.

You don't need to move to Tibet or enter a monastery to touch the secrets of stillness (thankfully). Instead, you simply need to find enough space in your life to let this mystical monk lead you by the hand closer to the heart of Jesus.

Steven James
Author of *Story: Recapture the Mystery*

BIOGRAPHY OF THOMAS À KEMPIS

Full Name: Thomas Hemerken (means "little hammer")

Date of Birth: 1379 or 1380 CE

Family Stats: His mother, Gertrude, kept the village school, and his father, John, most likely worked in metals. His brother John was at the Augustinian convent of Mount Saint Agnes before Thomas was.

Lived In: Born at Kempen, in the Diocese of Cologne (Germany); went to school in Deventer, in the Netherlands; his convent was Mount Saint Agnes, near Zwolle, also in the Netherlands.

Occupation: German monk, who worked mainly as a copyist; he joined the Augustinian canons in 1399, was ordained a priest c.1413, and made a subprior in 1429

Claim to Fame: His book, *The Imitation of Christ*, is one of the most well-known Christian books on devotion.

Famous Quote: "If thou wilt receive profit, read with humility, simplicity and faith, and seek not at any time the fame of being learned."

Famous Works: *The Imitation of Christ* is his most famous work. His writings are all devotional in character and include tracts and meditations, letters, sermons, and biographies.

Died: July 25, 1471, near Zwolle

Conversion Experience: While he was at school in Deventer, Thomas was much influenced by the "new devotion" encouraged by the school leaders. This devotion centered on the sincerity and enthusiasm associated with Christianity in the first century after Christ.

Miscellaneous Fact: He copied the Bible no less than four times; one of these copies is preserved at Darmstadt in five volumes.

CHAPTER I.

Imitating Christ and Despising All Vanities on Earth

"HE WHO follows Me, walks not in darkness," says the Lord.[1] By these words of Christ we are advised to imitate His life and habits, if we wish to be truly enlightened and free from all blindness of heart. Let our chief effort, therefore, be to study the life of Jesus Christ.

The teaching of Christ is more excellent than all the advice of the saints, and he who has His spirit will find in it a hidden manna. Now, there are many who hear the Gospel often but care little for it because they have not the spirit of Christ. Yet whoever wishes to understand fully the words of Christ must try to pattern his whole life on that of Christ.

What good does it do to speak learnedly about the Trinity if, lacking humility, you displease the Trinity? Indeed it is not learning that makes a man holy and just, but a virtuous life makes him pleasing to God. I would rather feel contrition than know how to define it. For what would it profit us to know the whole Bible by heart and the principles of all the philosophers if we live without grace and the love of God? Vanity of vanities and all is vanity, except to love God and serve Him alone.

This is the greatest wisdom—to seek the kingdom of heaven through contempt of the world. It is vanity, therefore, to seek and trust in riches that perish. It is vanity also to court honor and to be puffed up with pride. It is vanity to follow the lusts of the body and to desire things for which severe punishment later must come. It is vanity to wish for long life and to care little about a well-spent life. It is vanity to be concerned with the present only and not to make provision for things to come. It is vanity to love what passes quickly and not to look ahead where eternal joy abides.

Often recall the proverb: "The eye is not satisfied with seeing nor the ear filled with hearing."[2] Try, moreover, to turn your heart from the love of things visible and bring yourself to things invisible. For they who follow their own evil passions stain their consciences and lose the grace of God.

CHAPTER II.

Having a Humble Opinion of Self

EVERY man naturally desires knowledge[3]; but what good is knowledge without fear of God? Indeed a humble rustic who serves God is better than a proud intellectual who neglects his soul to study the course of the stars.[4] He who knows himself well becomes mean in his own eyes and is not happy when praised by men.

If I knew all things in the world and had not charity, what would it profit me before God Who will judge me by my deeds?

Shun too great a desire for knowledge, for in it there is much fretting and delusion. Intellectuals like to appear learned and to be called wise. Yet there are many things the knowledge of which does little or no good to the soul, and he who concerns himself about other things than those which lead to salvation is very unwise.

Many words do not satisfy the soul; but a good life eases the mind and a clean conscience inspires great trust in God.

The more you know and the better you understand, the more severely will you be judged, unless your life is also the more holy. Do not be proud, therefore, because of your learning or skill. Rather, fear because of the talent given you. If you think you know many things and understand them well enough, realize at the same time that there is much you do not know. Hence, do not affect wisdom, but admit your ignorance. Why prefer yourself to anyone else when many are more learned, more cultured than you?

If you wish to learn and appreciate something worth while, then love to be unknown and considered as nothing. Truly to know and despise self is the best and most perfect counsel. To think of oneself as nothing, and always to think well and highly of others is the best and most perfect wisdom. Wherefore, if you see another sin openly or commit a serious crime, do not consider yourself better, for you do not know how long you can remain in good estate. All men are frail, but you must admit that none is more frail than yourself.

CHAPTER III.

The Doctrine of Truth

HAPPY is he to whom truth manifests itself, not in signs and words that fade, but as it actually is. Our opinions, our senses often deceive us and we discern very little.

What good is much discussion of involved and obscure matters when our ignorance of them will not be held against us on Judgment Day? Neglect of things which are profitable and necessary and undue concern with those which are irrelevant and harmful, are great folly. We have eyes and do not see.

What, therefore, have we to do with questions of philosophy? He to whom the Eternal Word speaks is free from theorizing. For from this Word are all things and of Him all things speak—the Beginning Who also speaks to us. Without this Word no man understands or judges aright. He to whom it becomes everything, who traces all things to it and who sees all things in it, may ease his heart and remain at peace with God.

O God, You Who are the truth, make me one with

You in love everlasting. I am often wearied by the many things I hear and read, but in You is all that I long for. Let the learned be still, let all creatures be silent before You; You alone speak to me.

The more recollected a man is, and the more simple of heart he becomes, the easier he understands sublime things, for he receives the light of knowledge from above. The pure, simple, and steadfast spirit is not distracted by many labors, for he does them all for the honor of God. And since he enjoys interior peace he seeks no selfish end in anything. What, indeed, gives more trouble and affliction than uncontrolled desires of the heart?

A good and devout man arranges in his mind the things he has to do, not according to the whims of evil inclination but according to the dictates of right reason. Who is forced to struggle more than he who tries to master himself? This ought to be our purpose, then: to conquer self, to become stronger each day, to advance in virtue.

Every perfection in this life has some imperfection mixed with it and no learning of ours is without some darkness. Humble knowledge of self is a surer path to God than the ardent pursuit of learning. Not that learning is to be considered evil, or knowledge, which is good in itself and so ordained by God; but a clean conscience and virtuous life ought always to be preferred. Many often err and accomplish little or nothing because they try to become learned rather than to live well.

If men used as much care in uprooting vices and implanting virtues as they do in discussing problems, there would not be so much evil and scandal in the world, or such laxity in religious organizations. On the day of judgment, surely, we shall not be asked what we have read but what we have done; not how well we have spoken but how well we have lived.

Tell me, where now are all the masters and teachers whom you knew so well in life and who were famous for their learning? Others have already taken their places and I know not whether they ever think of their predecessors. During life they seemed to be something; now they are seldom remembered. How quickly the glory of the world passes away! If only their lives had kept pace with their learning, then their study and reading would have been worth while.

How many there are who perish because of vain worldly knowledge and too little care for serving God. They became vain in their own conceits because they chose to be great rather than humble.

He is truly great who has great charity. He is truly great who is little in his own eyes and makes nothing of the highest honor. He is truly wise who looks upon all earthly things as folly that he may gain Christ. He who does God's will and renounces his own is truly very learned.

CHAPTER IV.

Prudence in Action

DO NOT yield to every impulse and suggestion but consider things carefully and patiently in the light of God's will. For very often, sad to say, we are so weak that we believe and speak evil of others rather than good. Perfect men, however, do not readily believe every talebearer, because they know that human frailty is prone to evil and is likely to appear in speech.

Not to act rashly or to cling obstinately to one's opinion, not to believe everything people say or to spread abroad the gossip one has heard, is great wisdom.

Take counsel with a wise and conscientious man.

Seek the advice of your betters in preference to following your own inclinations.

A good life makes a man wise according to God and gives him experience in many things, for the more humble he is and the more subject to God, the wiser and the more at peace he will be in all things.

CHAPTER V.

Reading the Holy Scripture

TRUTH, not eloquence, is to be sought in reading the Holy Scriptures; and every part must be read in the spirit in which it was written. For in the Scriptures we ought to seek profit rather than polished diction.

Likewise we ought to read simple and devout books as willingly as learned and profound ones. We ought not to be swayed by the authority of the writer, whether he be a great literary light or an insignificant person, but by the love of simple truth. We ought not to ask who is speaking, but mark what is said. Men pass away, but the truth of the Lord remains forever. God speaks to us in many ways without regard for persons.

Our curiosity often impedes our reading of the Scriptures, when we wish to understand and mull over what we ought simply to read and pass by.

If you would profit from it, therefore, read with humility, simplicity, and faith, and never seek a reputation for being learned. Seek willingly and listen attentively to the words of the saints; do not be displeased with the sayings of the ancients, for they were not made without purpose.

CHAPTER VI.

Unbridled Affections

WHEN a man desires a thing too much, he at once becomes ill at ease. A proud and avaricious man never rests, whereas he who is poor and humble of heart lives in a world of peace. An unmortified man is quickly tempted and overcome in small, trifling evils; his spirit is weak, in a measure carnal and inclined to sensual things; he can hardly abstain from earthly desires. Hence it makes him sad to forego them; he is quick to anger if reproved. Yet if he satisfies his desires, remorse of conscience overwhelms him because he followed his passions and they did not lead to the peace he sought.

True peace of heart, then, is found in resisting passions, not in satisfying them. There is no peace in the carnal man, in the man given to vain attractions, but there is peace in the fervent and spiritual man.

CHAPTER VII.

Avoiding False Hope and Pride

VAIN is the man who puts his trust in men, in created things.

Do not be ashamed to serve others for the love of Jesus Christ and to seem poor in this world. Do not be self-sufficient but place your trust in God. Do what lies in your power and God will aid your good will. Put no trust in your own learning nor in the cunning of any man, but rather in the grace of God Who helps the humble and humbles the proud.

If you have wealth, do not glory in it, nor in friends because they are powerful, but in God Who gives all things and Who desires above all to give Himself. Do not boast of personal stature or of physical beauty, qualities which are marred and destroyed by a little sickness. Do not take pride in your talent or ability, lest you displease God to Whom belongs all the natural gifts that you have.

Do not think yourself better than others lest, perhaps,

you be accounted worse before God Who knows what is in man. Do not take pride in your good deeds, for God's judgments differ from those of men and what pleases them often displeases Him. If there is good in you, see more good in others, so that you may remain humble. It does no harm to esteem yourself less than anyone else, but it is very harmful to think yourself better than even one. The humble live in continuous peace, while in the hearts of the proud are envy and frequent anger.

CHAPTER VIII.

Shunning Over-Familiarity

DO NOT open your heart to every man, but discuss your affairs with one who is wise and who fears God. Do not keep company with young people and strangers. Do not fawn upon the rich, and do not be fond of mingling with the great. Associate with the humble and the simple, with the devout and virtuous, and with them speak of edifying things. Be not intimate with any woman, but generally commend all good women to God. Seek only the intimacy of God and of His angels, and avoid the notice of men.

We ought to have charity for all men but familiarity with all is not expedient. Sometimes it happens that a person enjoys a good reputation among those who do not know him, but at the same time is held in slight regard by those who do. Frequently we think we are pleasing others by our presence and we begin rather to displease them by the faults they find in us.

CHAPTER IX.

Obedience and Subjection

IT IS a very great thing to obey, to live under a superior and not to be one's own master, for it is much safer to be subject than it is to command. Many live in obedience more from necessity than from love. Such become discontented and dejected on the slightest pretext; they will never gain peace of mind unless they subject themselves wholeheartedly for the love of God.

Go where you may, you will find no rest except in humble obedience to the rule of authority. Dreams of happiness expected from change and different places have deceived many.

Everyone, it is true, wishes to do as he pleases and is attracted to those who agree with him. But if God be among us, we must at times give up our opinions for the blessings of peace.

Furthermore, who is so wise that he can have full knowledge of everything? Do not trust too much in your own opinions, but be willing to listen to those of others. If, though your own be good, you accept another's opinion for love of God, you will gain much more merit; for I have often heard that it is safer to listen to advice and take it than to give it. It may happen, too, that while one's own opinion may be good, refusal to agree with others when reason and occasion demand it, is a sign of pride and obstinacy.

CHAPTER X.

Avoiding Idle Talk

SHUN the gossip of men as much as possible, for discussion of worldly affairs, even though sincere, is a great distraction inasmuch as we are quickly ensnared and captivated by vanity.

Many a time I wish that I had held my peace and had not associated with men. Why, indeed, do we converse and gossip among ourselves when we so seldom part without a troubled conscience? We do so because we seek comfort from one another's conversation and wish to ease the mind wearied by diverse thoughts. Hence, we talk and think quite fondly of things we like very much or of things we dislike intensely. But, sad to say, we often talk vainly and to no purpose; for this external pleasure effectively bars inward and divine consolation.

Therefore we must watch and pray lest time pass idly.

When the right and opportune moment comes for speaking, say something that will edify.

Bad habits and indifference to spiritual progress do much to remove the guard from the tongue. Devout conversation on spiritual matters, on the contrary, is a great aid to spiritual progress, especially when persons of the same mind and spirit associate together in God.

CHAPTER XI.

Acquiring Peace and Zeal for Perfection

WE SHOULD enjoy much peace if we did not concern ourselves with what others say and do, for these are no concern of ours. How can a man who meddles in affairs not his own, who seeks strange distractions, and who is little or seldom inwardly recollected, live long in peace?

Blessed are the simple of heart for they shall enjoy peace in abundance.

Why were some of the saints so perfect and so given to contemplation? Because they tried to mortify entirely in themselves all earthly desires, and thus they were able to attach themselves to God with all their heart and freely to concentrate their innermost thoughts.

We are too occupied with our own whims and fancies, too taken up with passing things. Rarely do we completely conquer even one vice, and we are not inflamed with the desire to improve ourselves day by day; hence, we remain cold and indifferent. If we mortified our bodies perfectly and allowed no distractions to enter our minds, we could appreciate divine things and experience something of heavenly contemplation.

The greatest obstacle, indeed, the only obstacle, is that we are not free from passions and lusts, that we do not try to follow the perfect way of the saints. Thus when we encounter some slight difficulty, we are too easily dejected and turn to human consolations. If we tried, however, to stand as brave men in battle, the help of the Lord from heaven would surely sustain us. For He Who gives us the opportunity of fighting for victory, is ready to help those who carry on and trust in His grace.

If we let our progress in religious life depend on the observance of its externals alone, our devotion will quickly come to an end. Let us, then, lay the ax to the root that we may be freed from our passions and thus have peace of mind.

If we were to uproot only one vice each year, we should soon become perfect. The contrary, however, is often the case—we feel that we were better and purer in the first fervor of our conversion than we are after many years in the practice of our faith. Our fervor and progress ought to increase day by day; yet it is now considered noteworthy if a man can retain even a part of his first fervor.

If we did a little violence to ourselves at the start, we should afterwards be able to do all things with ease and joy. It is hard to break old habits, but harder still to go against our will.

If you do not overcome small, trifling things, how will you overcome the more difficult? Resist temptations in the beginning, and unlearn the evil habit lest perhaps, little by little, it lead to a more evil one.

If you but consider what peace a good life will bring to yourself and what joy it will give to others, I think you will be more concerned about your spiritual progress.

CHAPTER XII.

The Value of Adversity

IT IS good for us to have trials and troubles at times, for they often remind us that we are on probation and ought not to hope in any worldly thing. It is good for us sometimes to suffer contradiction, to be misjudged by men even though we do well and mean well. These things help us to be humble and shield us from vainglory. When to all outward appearances men give us no credit, when they do not think well of us, then we are more inclined to seek God Who sees our hearts. Therefore, a man ought to root himself so firmly in God that he will not need the consolations of men.

When a man of good will is afflicted, tempted, and tormented by evil thoughts, he realizes clearly that his greatest need is God, without Whom he can do no good. Saddened by his miseries and sufferings, he laments and prays. He wearies of living longer and wishes for death that he might be dissolved and be with Christ. Then he understands fully that perfect security and complete peace cannot be found on earth.

CHAPTER XIII.

Resisting Temptation

SO LONG as we live in this world we cannot escape suffering and temptation. Whence it is written in Job: "The life of man upon earth is a warfare."[5] Everyone, therefore, must guard against temptation and must watch in prayer lest the devil, who never sleeps but goes about seeking whom he may devour, find occasion to deceive him. No one is so perfect or so holy but he is sometimes tempted; man cannot be altogether free from temptation.

Yet temptations, though troublesome and severe, are often useful to a man, for in them he is humbled, purified, and instructed. The saints all passed through many temptations and trials to profit by them, while those who could not resist became reprobate and fell away. There is no state so holy, no place so secret that temptations and trials will not come. Man is never safe from them as long as he lives, for they come from within us—in sin we were born. When one temptation or trial passes, another comes; we shall always have something to suffer because we have lost the state of original blessedness.

Many people try to escape temptations, only to fall more deeply. We cannot conquer simply by fleeing, but by patience and true humility we become stronger than all our enemies. The man who only shuns temptations outwardly and does not uproot them will make little progress; indeed they will quickly return, more violent than before.

Little by little, in patience and long-suffering you will overcome them, by the help of God rather than by severity and your own rash ways. Often take counsel when tempted; and do not be harsh with others who are tempted, but console them as you yourself would wish to be consoled.

The beginning of all temptation lies in a wavering mind and little trust in God, for as a rudderless ship is driven hither and yon by waves, so a careless and irresolute man is tempted in many ways. Fire tempers iron and temptation steels the just. Often we do not know what we can stand, but temptation shows us what we are.

Above all, we must be especially alert against the beginnings of temptation, for the enemy is more easily conquered if he is refused admittance to the mind and is met beyond the threshold when he knocks.

Someone has said very aptly: "Resist the beginnings; remedies come too late, when by long delay the evil has gained strength." First, a mere thought comes to mind, then strong imagination, followed by pleasure, evil delight, and consent. Thus, because he is not resisted in the beginning, Satan gains full entry. And the longer a man delays in resisting, so much the weaker does he become each day, while the strength of the enemy grows against him.

Some suffer great temptations in the beginning of their conversion, others toward the end, while some are troubled almost constantly throughout their life. Others, again, are tempted but lightly according to the wisdom and justice of Divine Providence Who weighs the status and merit of each and prepares all for the salvation of His elect.

We should not despair, therefore, when we are tempted, but pray to God the more fervently that He may see fit to help us, for according to the word of Paul, He will make issue with temptation that we may be able to bear it. Let us humble our souls under the hand of God in every trial and temptation for He will save and exalt the humble in spirit.

In temptations and trials the progress of a man is measured; in them opportunity for merit and virtue is made more manifest.

When a man is not troubled it is not hard for him to be fervent and devout, but if he bears up patiently in time of adversity, there is hope for great progress.

Some, guarded against great temptations, are frequently overcome by small ones in order that, humbled by their weakness in small trials, they may not presume on their own strength in great ones.

CHAPTER XIV.

Avoiding Rash Judgment

TURN your attention upon yourself and beware of judging the deeds of other men, for in judging others a man labors vainly, often makes mistakes, and easily sins; whereas, in judging and taking stock of himself he does something that is always profitable.

We frequently judge that things are as we wish them to be, for through personal feeling true perspective is easily lost.

If God were the sole object of our desire, we should not be disturbed so easily by opposition to our opinions. But often something lurks within or happens from without to draw us along with it.

Many, unawares, seek themselves in the things they do. They seem even to enjoy peace of mind when things happen according to their wish and liking, but if otherwise than they desire, they are soon disturbed and saddened. Differences of feeling and opinion often divide friends and acquaintances, even those who are religious and devout.

An old habit is hard to break, and no one is willing to be led farther than he can see.

If you rely more upon your intelligence or industry than upon the virtue of submission to Jesus Christ, you will hardly, and in any case slowly, become an enlightened man. God wants us to be completely subject to Him and, through ardent love, to rise above all human wisdom.

CHAPTER XV.

Works Done in Charity

NEVER do evil for anything in the world, or for the love of any man. For one who is in need, however, a good work may at times be purposely left undone or changed for a better one. This is not the omission of a good deed but rather its improvement.

Without charity external work is of no value, but anything done in charity, be it ever so small and trivial, is entirely fruitful inasmuch as God weighs the love with which a man acts rather than the deed itself.

He does much who loves much. He does much who does a thing well. He does well who serves the common good rather than his own interests.

Now, that which seems to be charity is oftentimes really sensuality, for man's own inclination, his own will, his hope of reward, and his self-interest, are motives seldom absent. On the contrary, he who has true and perfect charity seeks self in nothing, but searches all things for the glory of God. Moreover, he envies no man, because he desires no personal pleasure nor does he wish to rejoice in himself; rather he desires the greater glory of God above all things. He ascribes to man nothing that is good but attributes it wholly to God from Whom all things proceed as from a fountain, and in Whom all the blessed shall rest as their last end and fruition.

If man had but a spark of true charity he would surely sense that all the things of earth are full of vanity!

CHAPTER XVI.

Bearing with the Faults of Others

UNTIL God ordains otherwise, a man ought to bear patiently whatever he cannot correct in himself and in others. Consider it better thus—perhaps to try your patience and to test you, for without such patience and trial your merits are of little account. Nevertheless, under such difficulties you should pray that God will consent to help you bear them calmly.

If, after being admonished once or twice, a person does not amend, do not argue with him but commit the whole matter to God that His will and honor may be furthered in all His servants, for God knows well how to turn evil to good. Try to bear patiently with the defects and infirmities of others, whatever they may be, because you also have many a fault which others must endure.

If you cannot make yourself what you would wish to be, how can you bend others to your will? We want them to be perfect, yet we do not correct our own faults. We wish them to be severely corrected, yet we will not correct ourselves. Their great liberty displeases us, yet we would not be denied what we ask. We would have them bound by laws, yet we will allow ourselves to be restrained in nothing. Hence, it is clear how seldom we think of others as we do of ourselves.

If all were perfect, what should we have to suffer from others for God's sake? But God has so ordained, that we may learn to bear with one another's burdens, for there is no man without fault, no man without burden, no man sufficient to himself nor wise enough. Hence we must support one another, console one another, mutually help, counsel, and advise, for the measure of every man's virtue is best revealed in time of adversity—adversity that does not weaken a man but rather shows what he is.

CHAPTER XVII.

Monastic Life

IF YOU wish peace and concord with others, you must learn to break your will in many things. To live in monasteries or religious communities, to remain there without complaint, and to persevere faithfully till death is no small matter.

Blessed indeed is he who there lives a good life and there ends his days in happiness.

If you would persevere in seeking perfection, you must consider yourself a pilgrim, an exile on earth. If you would become a religious, you must be content to seem a fool for the sake of Christ. Habit and tonsure change a man but little; it is the change of life, the complete mortification of passions that endow a true religious.

He who seeks anything but God alone and the salvation of his soul will find only trouble and grief, and he who does not try to become the least, the servant of all, cannot remain at peace for long.

You have come to serve, not to rule. You must understand, too, that you have been called to suffer and to work, not to idle and gossip away your time. Here men are tried as gold in a furnace. Here no man can remain unless he desires with all his heart to humble himself before God.

CHAPTER XVIII.

The Example Set Us
by the Holy Fathers

CONSIDER the lively examples set us by the saints, who possessed the light of true perfection and religion, and you will see how little, how nearly nothing, we do. What, alas, is our life, compared with theirs? The saints and friends of Christ served the Lord in hunger and thirst, in cold and nakedness, in work and fatigue, in vigils and fasts, in prayers and holy meditations, in persecutions and many afflictions. How many and severe were the trials they suffered—the Apostles, martyrs, confessors, virgins, and all the rest who willed to follow in the footsteps of Christ! They hated their lives on earth that they might have life in eternity.

How strict and detached were the lives the holy hermits led in the desert! What long and grave temptations they suffered! How often were they beset by the enemy! What frequent and ardent prayers they offered to God! What rigorous fasts they observed! How great their zeal and their love for spiritual perfection! How brave the fight they waged to master their evil habits! What pure and straightforward purpose they showed toward God! By day they labored and by night they spent themselves in long prayers. Even at work they did not cease from mental prayer. They used all their time profitably; every hour seemed too short for serving God, and in the great sweetness of contemplation, they forgot even their bodily needs.

They renounced all riches, dignities, honors, friends, and associates. They desired nothing of the world. They scarcely allowed themselves the necessities of life, and the service of the body, even when necessary, was irksome to them. They were poor in earthly things but rich in grace and virtue. Outwardly destitute, inwardly they were full of grace and divine consolation. Strangers to the world, they were close and intimate friends of God. To themselves they seemed as nothing, and they were despised by the world, but in the eyes of God they were precious and beloved. They lived in true humility and simple obedience; they walked in charity and patience, making progress daily on the pathway of spiritual life and obtaining great favor with God.

They were given as an example for all religious, and their power to stimulate us to perfection ought to be greater than that of the lukewarm to tempt us to laxity.

How great was the fervor of all religious in the beginning

of their holy institution! How great their devotion in prayer and their rivalry for virtue! What splendid discipline flourished among them! What great reverence and obedience in all things under the rule of a superior! The footsteps they left behind still bear witness that they indeed were holy and perfect men who fought bravely and conquered the world.

Today, he who is not a transgressor and who can bear patiently the duties which he has taken upon himself is considered great. How lukewarm and negligent we are! We lose our original fervor very quickly and we even become weary of life from laziness! Do not you, who have seen so many examples of the devout, fall asleep in the pursuit of virtue!

CHAPTER XIX.

The Practices of a Good Religious

THE life of a good religious ought to abound in every virtue so that he is interiorly what to others he appears to be. With good reason there ought to be much more within than appears on the outside, for He who sees within is God, Whom we ought to reverence most highly wherever we are and in Whose sight we ought to walk pure as the angels.

Each day we ought to renew our resolutions and arouse ourselves to fervor as though it were the first day of our religious life. We ought to say: "Help me, O Lord God, in my good resolution and in Your holy service. Grant me now, this very day, to begin perfectly, for thus far I have done nothing."

As our intention is, so will be our progress; and he who desires perfection must be very diligent. If the strong-willed man fails frequently, what of the man who makes up his mind seldom or half-heartedly? Many are the ways of failing in our resolutions; even a slight omission of religious practice entails a loss of some kind.

Just men depend on the grace of God rather than on their own wisdom in keeping their resolutions. In Him they confide every undertaking, for man, indeed, proposes but God disposes, and God's way is not man's. If a habitual exercise is sometimes omitted out of piety or in the interests of another, it can easily be resumed later. But if it be abandoned carelessly, through weariness or neglect, then the fault is great and will prove hurtful. Much as we try, we still fail too easily in many things. Yet we must always have some fixed purpose, especially against things which beset us the most. Our outward and inward lives alike must be closely watched and well ordered, for both are important to perfection.

If you cannot recollect yourself continuously, do so once a day at least, in the morning or in the evening. In the morning make a resolution and in the evening examine yourself on what you have said this day, what you have done and thought, for in these things perhaps you have often offended God and those about you.

Arm yourself like a man against the devil's assaults. Curb your appetite and you will more easily curb every inclination of the flesh. Never be completely unoccupied, but read or write or pray or meditate or do something for the common good. Bodily discipline, however, must be undertaken with discretion and is not to be practiced indiscriminately by everyone.

Devotions not common to all are not to be displayed in public, for such personal things are better performed in private. Furthermore, beware of indifference to community prayer through love of your own devotions. If, however, after doing completely and faithfully all you are bound and commanded to do, you then have leisure, use it as personal piety suggests.

Not everyone can have the same devotion. One exactly suits this person, another that. Different exercises, likewise, are suitable for different times, some for feast days and some again for weekdays. In time of temptation we need certain devotions. For days of rest and peace we need others. Some are suitable when we are sad, others when we are joyful in the Lord.

About the time of the principal feasts good devotions ought to be renewed and the intercession of the saints more fervently implored. From one feast day to the next we ought to fix our purpose as though we were then to pass from this world and come to the eternal holyday.

During holy seasons, finally, we ought to prepare ourselves carefully, to live holier lives, and to observe each rule more strictly, as though we were soon to receive from God the reward of our labors. If this end be deferred, let us believe that we are not well prepared and that we are not yet worthy of the great glory that shall in due time be revealed to us. Let us try, meanwhile, to prepare ourselves better for death.

"Blessed is the servant," says Christ, "whom his master, when he cometh, shall find watching. Amen I say to you: he shall make him ruler over all his goods."[6]

CHAPTER XX.

The Love of Solitude and Silence

SEEK a suitable time for leisure and meditate often on the favors of God. Leave curiosities alone. Read such matters as bring sorrow to the heart rather than occupation to the mind. If you withdraw yourself from unnecessary talking and idle running about, from listening to gossip and rumors, you will find enough time that is suitable for holy meditation.

Very many great saints avoided the company of men wherever possible and chose to serve God in retirement. "As often as I have been among men," said one writer, "I have returned less a man." We often find this to be true when we take part in long conversations. It is easier to be silent altogether than not to speak too much. To stay at home is easier than to be sufficiently on guard while away. Anyone, then, who aims to live the inner and spiritual life must go apart, with Jesus, from the crowd.

No man appears in safety before the public eye unless he first relishes obscurity. No man is safe in speaking unless he loves to be silent. No man rules safely unless he is willing to be ruled. No man commands safely unless he has learned well how to obey. No man rejoices safely unless he has within him the testimony of a good conscience.

More than this, the security of the saints was always enveloped in the fear of God, nor were they less cautious and humble because they were conspicuous for great virtues and graces. The security of the wicked, on the contrary, springs from pride and presumption, and will end in their own deception.

Never promise yourself security in this life, even though you seem to be a good religious, or a devout hermit. It happens very often that those whom men esteem highly are more seriously endangered by their own excessive confidence. Hence, for many it is better not to be too free from temptations, but often to be tried lest they become too secure, too filled with pride, or even too eager to fall back upon external comforts.

If only a man would never seek passing joys or entangle himself with worldly affairs, what a good conscience he would have. What great peace and tranquillity would be his, if he cut himself off from all empty care and thought only of things divine, things helpful to his soul, and put all his trust in God.

No man deserves the consolation of heaven unless he persistently arouses himself to holy contrition.

If you desire true sorrow of heart, seek the privacy of your cell and shut out the uproar of the world, as it is written: "In your chamber bewail your sins." There you will find what too often you lose abroad.

Your cell will become dear to you if you remain in it, but if you do not, it will become wearisome. If in the beginning of your religious life, you live within your cell and keep to it, it will soon become a special friend and a very great comfort.

In silence and quiet the devout soul advances in virtue and learns the hidden truths of Scripture. There she finds a flood of tears with which to bathe and cleanse herself nightly, that she may become the more intimate with her Creator the farther she withdraws from all the tumult of the world. For God and His holy angels will draw near to him who withdraws from friends and acquaintances.

It is better for a man to be obscure and to attend to his salvation than to neglect it and work miracles. It is praiseworthy for a religious seldom to go abroad, to flee the sight of men and have no wish to see them.

Why wish to see what you are not permitted to have? "The world passes away and the concupiscence thereof." Sensual craving sometimes entices you to wander around, but when the moment is past, what do you bring back with you save a disturbed conscience and heavy heart? A happy going often leads to a sad return, a merry evening to a mournful dawn. Thus, all carnal joy begins sweetly but in the end brings remorse and death.

What can you find elsewhere that you cannot find here in your cell? Behold heaven and earth and all the elements, for of these all things are made. What can you see anywhere under the sun that will remain long? Perhaps you think you will completely satisfy yourself, but you cannot do so, for if you should see all existing things, what would they be but an empty vision?

Raise your eyes to God in heaven and pray because of your sins and shortcomings. Leave vanity to the vain. Set yourself to the things which God has commanded you to do. Close the door upon yourself and call to you Jesus, your Beloved. Remain with Him in your cell, for nowhere else will you find such peace. If you had not left it, and had not listened to idle gossip, you would have remained in greater peace. But since you love, sometimes, to hear news, it is only right that you should suffer sorrow of heart from it.

CHAPTER XXI.

Sorrow of Heart

IF YOU wish to make progress in virtue, live in the fear of the Lord, do not look for too much freedom, discipline your senses, and shun inane silliness. Sorrow opens the door to many a blessing which dissoluteness usually destroys.

It is a wonder that any man who considers and meditates on his exiled state and the many dangers to his soul, can ever be perfectly happy in this life. Lighthearted and heedless of our defects, we do not feel the real sorrows of our souls, but often indulge in empty laughter when we have good reason to weep. No liberty is true and no joy is genuine unless it is founded in the fear of the Lord and a good conscience.

Happy is the man who can throw off the weight of every care and recollect himself in holy contrition. Happy is the man who casts from him all that can stain or burden his conscience.

Fight like a man. Habit is overcome by habit. If you leave men alone, they will leave you alone to do what you have to do. Do not busy yourself about the affairs of others and do not become entangled in the business of your superiors. Keep an eye primarily on yourself and admonish yourself instead of your friends.

If you do not enjoy the favor of men, do not let it sadden you; but consider it a serious matter if you do not conduct yourself as well or as carefully as is becoming for a servant of God and a devout religious.

It is often better and safer for us to have few consolations in this life, especially comforts of the body. Yet if we do not have divine consolation or experience it rarely, it is our own fault because we seek no sorrow of heart and do not forsake vain outward satisfaction.

Consider yourself unworthy of divine solace and deserving rather of much tribulation. When a man is perfectly contrite, the whole world is bitter and wearisome to him.

A good man always finds enough over which to mourn and weep; whether he thinks of himself or of his neighbor he knows that no one lives here without suffering, and the closer he examines himself the more he grieves.

The sins and vices in which we are so entangled that

we can rarely apply ourselves to the contemplation of heaven are matters for just sorrow and inner remorse.

I do not doubt that you would correct yourself more earnestly if you would think more of an early death than of a long life. And if you pondered in your heart the future pains of hell or of purgatory, I believe you would willingly endure labor and trouble and would fear no hardship. But since these thoughts never pierce the heart and since we are enamored of flattering pleasure, we remain very cold and indifferent. Our wretched body complains so easily because our soul is altogether too lifeless.

Pray humbly to the Lord, therefore, that He may give you the spirit of contrition and say with the Prophet: "Feed me, Lord, with the bread of mourning and give me to drink of tears in full measure."[7]

CHAPTER XXII.

Thoughts on the Misery of Man

WHEREVER you are, wherever you go, you are miserable unless you turn to God. So why be dismayed when things do not happen as you wish and desire? Is there anyone who has everything as he wishes? No—neither I, nor you, nor any man on earth. There is no one in the world, be he Pope or king, who does not suffer trial and anguish.

Who is the better off then? Surely, it is the man who will suffer something for God. Many unstable and weak-minded people say: "See how well that man lives, how rich, how great he is, how powerful and mighty." But you must lift up your eyes to the riches of heaven and realize that the material goods of which they speak are nothing. These things are uncertain and very burdensome because they are never possessed without anxiety and fear. Man's happiness does not consist in the possession of abundant goods; a very little is enough.

Living on earth is truly a misery. The more a man desires spiritual life, the more bitter the present becomes to him, because he understands better and sees more clearly the defects, the corruption of human nature. To eat and drink, to watch and sleep, to rest, to labor, and to be bound by other human necessities is certainly a great misery and affliction to the devout man, who would gladly be released from them and be free from all sin. Truly, the inner man is greatly burdened in this world by the necessities of the body, and for this reason the Prophet prayed that he might be as free from them as possible, when he said: "From my necessities, O Lord, deliver me."[8]

But woe to those who know not their own misery, and greater woe to those who love this miserable and corruptible life. Some, indeed, can scarcely procure its necessities either by work or by begging; yet they love it so much that, if they could live here always, they would care nothing for the kingdom of God.

How foolish and faithless of heart are those who are so engrossed in earthly things as to relish nothing but what is carnal! Miserable men indeed, for in the end they will see to their sorrow how cheap and worthless was the thing they loved.

The saints of God and all devout friends of Christ did not look to what pleases the body nor to the things that are popular from time to time. Their whole hope and aim centered on the everlasting good. Their whole desire pointed upward to the lasting and invisible realm, lest the love of what is visible drag them down to lower things.

Do not lose heart, then, my brother, in pursuing your spiritual life. There is yet time, and your hour is not past. Why delay your purpose? Arise! Begin at once and say: "Now is the time to act, now is the time to fight, now is the proper time to amend."

When you are troubled and afflicted, that is the time to gain merit. You must pass through water and fire before coming to rest. Unless you do violence to yourself you will not overcome vice.

So long as we live in this fragile body, we can neither be free from sin nor live without weariness and sorrow. Gladly would we rest from all misery, but in losing innocence through sin we also lost true blessedness. Therefore, we must have patience and await the mercy of God until this iniquity passes, until mortality is swallowed up in life.

How great is the frailty of human nature which is ever prone to evil! Today you confess your sins and tomorrow you again commit the sins which you confessed. One moment you resolve to be careful, and yet after an hour you act as though you had made no resolution.

We have cause, therefore, because of our frailty and feebleness, to humble ourselves and never think anything great of ourselves. Through neglect we may quickly lose that which by God's grace we have acquired only through long, hard labor. What, eventually, will become of us who so quickly grow lukewarm? Woe to us if we presume to rest in peace and security when actually there is no true holiness in our lives. It would be beneficial for us, like good novices, to be instructed once more in the principles of a good life, to see if there be hope of amendment and greater spiritual progress in the future.

CHAPTER XXIII.

Thoughts on Death

VERY soon your life here will end; consider, then, what may be in store for you elsewhere. Today we live; tomorrow we die and are quickly forgotten. Oh, the dullness and hardness of a heart which looks only to the present instead of preparing for that which is to come! Therefore, in every deed and every thought, act as though you were to die this very day. If you had a good conscience you would not fear death very much. It is better to avoid sin than to fear death. If you are not prepared today, how will you be prepared tomorrow? Tomorrow is an uncertain day; how do you know you will have a tomorrow?

What good is it to live a long life when we amend that life so little? Indeed, a long life does not always benefit us, but on the contrary, frequently adds to our guilt. Would that in this world we had lived well throughout one single day. Many count up the years they have spent in religion but find their lives made little holier. If it is so terrifying to die, it is nevertheless possible that to live longer is more dangerous. Blessed is he who keeps the moment of death ever before his eyes and prepares for it every day.

If you have ever seen a man die, remember that you, too, must go the same way. In the morning consider that you may not live till evening, and when evening comes do not dare to promise yourself the dawn. Be always ready, therefore, and so live that death will never take you unprepared. Many die suddenly and unexpectedly, for in the unexpected hour the Son of God will come. When that last moment arrives you will begin to have a quite different opinion of the life that is now entirely past and you will regret very much that you were so careless and remiss.

How happy and prudent is he who tries now in life to be what he wants to be found in death. Perfect contempt of the world, a lively desire to advance in virtue, a love for discipline, the works of penance, readiness to obey, self-denial, and the endurance of every hardship for the love of Christ, these will give a man great expectations of a happy death.

You can do many good works when in good health; what can you do when you are ill? Few are made better by sickness. Likewise they who undertake many pilgrimages seldom become holy.

Do not put your trust in friends and relatives, and do

not put off the care of your soul till later, for men will forget you more quickly than you think. It is better to provide now, in time, and send some good account ahead of you than to rely on the help of others. If you do not care for your own welfare now, who will care when you are gone?

The present is very precious; these are the days of salvation; now is the acceptable time. How sad that you do not spend the time in which you might purchase everlasting life in a better way. The time will come when you will want just one day, just one hour in which to make amends, and do you know whether you will obtain it?

See, then, dearly beloved, the great danger from which you can free yourself and the great fear from which you can be saved, if only you will always be wary and mindful of death. Try to live now in such a manner that at the moment of death you may be glad rather than fearful. Learn to die to the world now, that then you may begin to live with Christ. Learn to spurn all things now, that then you may freely go to Him. Chastise your body in penance now, that then you may have the confidence born of certainty.

Ah, foolish man, why do you plan to live long when you are not sure of living even a day? How many have been deceived and suddenly snatched away! How often have you heard of persons being killed by drownings, by fatal falls from high places, of persons dying at meals, at play, in fires, by the sword, in pestilence, or at the hands of robbers! Death is the end of everyone and the life of man quickly passes away like a shadow.

Who will remember you when you are dead? Who will pray for you? Do now, beloved, what you can, because you do not know when you will die, nor what your fate will be after death. Gather for yourself the riches of immortality while you have time. Think of nothing but your salvation. Care only for the things of God. Make friends for yourself now by honoring the saints of God, by imitating their actions, so that when you depart this life they may receive you into everlasting dwellings.

Keep yourself as a stranger here on earth, a pilgrim whom its affairs do not concern at all. Keep your heart free and raise it up to God, for you have not here a lasting home. To Him direct your daily prayers, your sighs and tears, that your soul may merit after death to pass in happiness to the Lord.

CHAPTER XXIV.

Judgment and the Punishment of Sin

IN ALL things consider the end; how you shall stand before the strict Judge from Whom nothing is hidden and Who will pronounce judgment in all justice, accepting neither bribes nor excuses. And you, miserable and wretched sinner, who fear even the countenance of an angry man, what answer will you make to the God Who knows all your sins? Why do you not provide for yourself against the day of judgment when no man can be excused or defended by another because each will have enough to do to answer for himself? In this life your work is profitable, your tears acceptable, your sighs audible, your sorrow satisfying and purifying.

The patient man goes through a great and salutary purgatory when he grieves more over the malice of one who harms him than for his own injury; when he prays readily for his enemies and forgives offenses from his heart; when he does not hesitate to ask pardon of others; when he is more easily moved to pity than to anger; when he does frequent violence to himself and tries to bring the body into complete subjection to the spirit.

It is better to atone for sin now and to cut away vices than to keep them for purgation in the hereafter.

In truth, we deceive ourselves by our ill-advised love of the flesh. What will that fire feed upon but our sins? The more we spare ourselves now and the more we satisfy the flesh, the harder will the reckoning be and the more we keep for the burning.

For a man will be more grievously punished in the things in which he has sinned. There the lazy will be driven with burning prongs, and gluttons tormented with unspeakable hunger and thirst; the wanton and lust-loving will be bathed in burning pitch and foul brimstone; the envious will howl in their grief like mad dogs.

Every vice will have its own proper punishment. The proud will be faced with every confusion and the avaricious pinched with the most abject want. One hour of suffering there will be more bitter than a hundred years of the most severe penance here. In this life men sometimes rest from work and enjoy the comfort of friends, but the damned have no rest or consolation.

You must, therefore, take care and repent of your sins now so that on the day of judgment you may rest secure with the blessed. For on that day the just will stand firm against those who tortured and oppressed them, and he who now submits humbly to the judgment of men will arise to pass judgment upon them. The poor and humble will have great confidence, while the proud will be struck with fear. He who learned to be a fool in this world and to be scorned for Christ will then appear to have been wise.

In that day every trial borne in patience will be pleasing and the voice of iniquity will be stilled; the devout will be glad; the irreligious will mourn; and the mortified body will rejoice far more than if it had been pampered with every pleasure. Then the cheap garment will shine with splendor and the rich one become faded and worn; the poor cottage will be more praised than the gilded palace. In that day persevering patience will count more than all the power in this world; simple obedience will be exalted above all worldly cleverness; a good and clean conscience will gladden the heart of man far more than the philosophy of the learned; and contempt for riches will be of more weight than every treasure on earth.

Then you will find more consolation in having prayed devoutly than in having fared daintily; you will be happy that you preferred silence to prolonged gossip.

Then holy works will be of greater value than many fair words; strictness of life and hard penances will be more pleasing than all earthly delights.

Learn, then, to suffer little things now that you may not have to suffer greater ones in eternity. Prove here what you can bear hereafter. If you can suffer only a little now, how will you be able to endure eternal torment? If a little suffering makes you impatient now, what will hell fire do? In truth, you cannot have two joys: you cannot taste the pleasures of this world and afterward reign with Christ.

If your life to this moment had been full of honors and pleasures, what good would it do if at this instant you should die? All is vanity, therefore, except to love God and to serve Him alone.

He who loves God with all his heart does not fear death or punishment or judgment or hell, because perfect love assures access to God.

It is no wonder that he who still delights in sin fears death and judgment.

It is good, however, that even if love does not as yet restrain you from evil, at least the fear of hell does. The man who casts aside the fear of God cannot continue long in goodness but will quickly fall into the snares of the devil.

CHAPTER XXV.

Zeal in Amending Our Lives

BE WATCHFUL and diligent in God's service and often think of why you left the world and came here. Was it not that you might live for God and become a spiritual man? Strive earnestly for perfection, then, because in a short time you will receive the reward of your labor, and neither fear nor sorrow shall come upon you at the hour of death.

Labor a little now, and soon you shall find great rest, in truth, eternal joy; for if you continue faithful and diligent in doing, God will undoubtedly be faithful and generous in rewarding. Continue to have reasonable hope of gaining salvation, but do not act as though you were certain of it lest you grow indolent and proud.

One day when a certain man who wavered often and anxiously between hope and fear was struck with sadness, he knelt in humble prayer before the altar of a church. While meditating on these things, he said: "Oh if I but knew whether I should persevere to the end!" Instantly he heard within the divine answer: "If you knew this, what would you do? Do now what you would do then and you will be quite secure." Immediately consoled and comforted, he resigned himself to the divine will and the anxious uncertainty ceased. His curiosity no longer sought to know what the future held for him, and he tried instead to find the perfect, the acceptable will of God in the beginning and end of every good work.

"Trust thou in the Lord and do good," says the Prophet; "dwell in the land and thou shalt feed on its riches."[9]

There is one thing that keeps many from zealously improving their lives, that is, dread of the difficulty, the toil of battle. Certainly they who try bravely to overcome the most difficult and unpleasant obstacles far outstrip others in the pursuit of virtue. A man makes the most progress and merits the most grace precisely in those matters wherein he gains the greatest victories over self and most mortifies his will. True, each one has his own difficulties to meet and conquer, but a diligent and sincere man will make greater progress even though he have more passions than one who is more even-tempered but less concerned about virtue.

Two things particularly further improvement—to withdraw oneself forcibly from those vices to which nature is viciously inclined, and to work fervently for those graces which are most needed.

Study also to guard against and to overcome the faults which in others very frequently displease you. Make the best of every opportunity, so that if you see or hear good example you may be moved to imitate it. On the other hand, take care lest you be guilty of those things which you consider reprehensible, or if you have ever been guilty of them, try to correct yourself as soon as possible. As you see others, so they see you.

How pleasant and sweet to behold brethren fervent and devout, well mannered and disciplined! How sad and painful to see them wandering in dissolution, not practicing the things to which they are called! How hurtful it is to neglect the purpose of their vocation and to attend to what is not their business!

Remember the purpose you have undertaken, and keep in mind the image of the Crucified. Even though you may have walked for many years on the pathway to God, you may well be ashamed if, with the image of Christ before you, you do not try to make yourself still more like Him.

The religious who concerns himself intently and devoutly with our Lord's most holy life and passion will find there an abundance of all things useful and necessary for him. He need not seek for anything better than Jesus.

If the Crucified should come to our hearts, how quickly and abundantly we would learn!

A fervent religious accepts all the things that are commanded him and does them well, but a negligent and lukewarm religious has trial upon trial, and suffers anguish from every side because he has no consolation within and is forbidden to seek it from without. The religious who does not live up to his rule exposes himself to dreadful ruin, and he who wishes to be more free and untrammeled will always be in trouble, for something or other will always displease him.

How do so many other religious who are confined in cloistered discipline get along? They seldom go out, they live in contemplation, their food is poor, their clothing coarse, they work hard, they speak but little, keep long vigils, rise early, pray much, read frequently, and subject themselves to all sorts of discipline. Think of the Carthusians and the Cistercians, the monks and nuns of different orders, how every night they rise to sing praise to the Lord. It would be a shame if you should grow lazy in such holy service when so many religious have already begun to rejoice in God.

If there were nothing else to do but praise the Lord God with all your heart and voice, if you had never to eat, or drink, or sleep, but could praise God always and occupy yourself solely with spiritual pursuits, how much happier you would be than you are now, a slave to every necessity of the body! Would that there were no such needs, but only the spiritual refreshments of the soul which, sad to say, we taste too seldom!

When a man reaches a point where he seeks no solace from any creature, then he begins to relish God perfectly. Then also he will be content no matter what may happen to him. He will neither rejoice over great things nor grieve over small ones, but will place himself entirely and confidently in the hands of God, Who for him is all in all, to Whom nothing ever perishes or dies, for Whom all things live, and Whom they serve as He desires.

Always remember your end and do not forget that lost time never returns. Without care and diligence you will never acquire virtue. When you begin to grow lukewarm, you are falling into the beginning of evil; but if you give yourself to fervor, you will find peace and will experience less hardship because of God's grace and the love of virtue.

A fervent and diligent man is ready for all things. It is greater work to resist vices and passions than to sweat in physical toil. He who does not overcome small faults, shall fall little by little into greater ones.

If you have spent the day profitably, you will always be happy at eventide. Watch over yourself, arouse yourself, warn yourself, and regardless of what becomes of others, do not neglect yourself. The more violence you do to yourself, the more progress you will make.

NOTES

CHAPTER I.
1. John 8:12
2. Eccles. 1:8

CHAPTER II.
3. Aristotle, *Metaphysics*, i. 1.
4. Augustine, *Confessions*, V. 4.

CHAPTER XIII.
5. Job 7:1.

CHAPTER XIX.
6. Luke 12:43, 44

CHAPTER XXI.
7. Ps. 79:6.

CHAPTER XXII.
8. Ps. 34:17

CHAPTER XXV.
9. Ps. 36:3.

[RELEVANT BOOKS]

FOR MORE INFORMATION ABOUT
OTHER RELEVANT BOOKS,

check out www.RELEVANTbooks.com.

Thomas à Kempis
THE IMITATION OF CHRIST

A profoundly influential masterpiece from 15th-century mystic Thomas à Kempis, *The Imitation of Christ* still resonates today. Deeply honest, spiritually challenging and often uncomfortably blunt, it calls believers away from materialism and self-absorption and toward a full-on commitment to the core of the Christian faith: living like Jesus. No wonder it's considered to be history's most-read Christian text apart from the Bible.

PRAISES THROUGH THE AGES

"Nothing more holy, nothing more honourable, nothing more religious, nothing more profitable for the Christian commonwealth can you ever do than to make known these works of Thomas à Kempis."
—PRIOR PIRKHAMER

"It is very profitable to read at times from the books of *The Imitation of Christ*, and of the Gospels and the Lives of the Saints."
—ST. IGNATIUS LOYOLA

CLASSIC CHRISTIAN WRITING FOR TODAY'S THINKER

In centuries past, influential Christian thinkers—radical, visionary pioneers of the faith—have penned literature that continues to influence Christians today. The Foundations of Faith series unearths these works for a new audience of twentysomethings hungry for revolutionary material that speaks to their lives. Rediscover the cornerstones of the Christian faith with these classic works.

OTHER TITLES FROM THE FOUNDATIONS OF FAITH SERIES

Saint Augustine
HANDBOOK ON FAITH, HOPE, AND LOVE

John Wesley
A PLAIN ACCOUNT OF CHRISTIAN PERFECTION

Charles Spurgeon
SELECTIONS FROM THE SPURGEON SERMON ARCHIVE

G.K. Chesterton
ORTHODOXY

Blaise Pascal
FOUNDATIONS OF THE CHRISTIAN RELIGION

Christian Living/ Spiritual Growth/ Spiritual Form
ISBN 0-9776167-1-1   **$8.99 USD**

[RELEVANTBOOKS]
WWW.RELEVANTBOOKS.COM